The Candle I Hold Up to See You

BOOKS BY CATHY SMITH BOWERS

The Love That Ended Yesterday in Texas

Traveling in Time of Danger

A Book of Minutes

The Candle I Hold Up to See You

Poems

Cathy Smith Bowers

Iris Press
Oak Ridge, Tennessee

Iris Press is an imprint of the Iris Publishing Group, Inc.
www.irisbooks.com

Book Design by Robert B. Cumming, Jr.

Library of Congress Cataloging-in-Publication Data

Bowers, Cathy Smith, 1949-
The candle I hold up to see you : poems / Cathy Smith Bowers.
    p. cm.
ISBN 978-1-60454-202-8 (pbk. : alk. paper)
I. Title.
PS3552.O871965C36 2009
811'.54—dc22

2009007143

ACKNOWLEDGMENTS

Asheville Poetry Review: "A Suit Our Brother Could Have Worn"

The Georgia Review: "The Napkin," "An American Family," "The Sabbatical"

English Journal: "Syntax," "Found Poem"

The Gettysburg Review: "Questions for Pluto," "Last Day," "The Notes," "How It Is in Their Clothes," "Pear Moonshine"

Nimrod: "Whistle-Speak"

Rapid River: "Solace," "Where's My Frog?," "All Adverbs, Adjectives Too"

Southern Poetry Anthology: "Shadow Dancing," "The Living Daylights," "First-Year Teacher"

Southern Poetry Review: "Cool Radio"

The Southern Review: "Abattoir," "Unmentionables," "Language: A Sentimental Education"

Wind: "My Brother's Star"

DEDICATION

I dedicate this book to all my earthly angels who held me in this world when I did not want to be here.

First, to my brother-in-law Clyde E. Buchanan, empirical evidence that God in one of his many incarnations drives a red truck. To my beloved and steadfast sisters and brother—Patricia Smith Buchanan, Rosemary Smith Tipton, and Allen Dale Smith. To my brother-in-law J.R. Tipton and sister-in-law Julie Davis Smith. To Carli Rose Buchanan and her creators, Noel and Brandi. To Heather Tipton. To Anna and Andy. To Jerry Rhodus. To Aunt Juanita.

To my cherished son and daughter—Jeff Stockdale and Jenny Stockdale.

To the real POETS in my life—Marsha Purvis, Charlotte Shaw, Lou Hayes, Debby Hegler, and Jim Mullis (posthumously).

To Gabe Purvis.

To my loyal friends and literary companions—Becky McClanahan and Gail Peck.

To my sisters in poetry—Eleanor Brawley, Ione O'Hara, Dede Wilson, Diana Pinckney, and Mary Martin. To Terri Wolfe and Louise Rockwell.

To my homey, my Fire, my partner in literary crime—Karon Gleaton Luddy.

To the faculty, staff, and students of The Haden Institute, especially Bob and Mary Ann Haden, Diana McEndree, Joyce Rockwood Hudson, Susan Sims Smith, Layne Rasche, and Chelsea Wakefield. To Joann Hassler, Rita Travis, and Karen Blaha.

To the faculty, staff, and students of Queens University of Charlotte, especially those in the low-residency MFA Program. Liz Strout, I love you bunches.

To Pam Hildebran.

To my Great Smokies' loves.

To John Lane and Betsy Teeter.

To the town of Tryon, NC, especially Tommy and Missy Lytle, Jay and Betsy Goree, Candy Butler, Sue Campbell, Sandy McCormack, Frances Smith, Dan and Angelica Ferebee (posthumously), Pat and Ike Wilson, Monica Jones and Terry Ackerman, and Jeff and Helen Byrd. And to all the guys at Trade Street Gallery Coffee House.

A special thanks—more than I could ever express—to Bob, Carmen and Beto Cumming.

Contents

Eight Names for God

A Sentimental Education

An American Family

UNMENTIONABLES

QUESTIONS FOR PLUTO

NOTES   89

*Speech is the candle I hold up to see you
and the night bent down to cup us in its giant hand.*

—Alan Shapiro, "Turn"

*Metaphor, after all, is neither
the candle nor the wick,
but the burning.*

—Thomas Hohstadt

Eight Names for God

וֵהוּ

This, the Kabbalah tells us,
is the first name of God.
With us from the beginning
in the darkened houses
of our beings, the switch
that was always there
waiting only
to be turned on.

The name that loves us so,
it will suffer us, unkind,
to go back in time, undo
before they do to us
our ancient crimes.

Cain's bruised and battered
fist once more unscathed.
Booth's yet unfired revolver
nestled in his vest.
Lizzie's axe returned
unbloodied to its shed.

Just rest your eyes, the book
instructs, on the untranslatable
beauty of each character.
Now look!

There's Able well among his flock again.
The Bordens bent content to their daily tasks.
And Abe, old Abe, in the high safe chamber
of his balcony—applauding—still.

יְלִי

Heavenly hurt, Miss Emily
called it, *imperial affliction
sent us of the air.* We've

all been there. Yet here
is the name that says we can
reclaim those sparks that once

emblazoned us. Like the stars
we walk beneath each night,
their own light dead for eons

we are told. Though there they are
above the browning ash and oak
strung high before our eyes

in the wintry limbs. Little
Promethei of our dampered souls,
go forth, go forth, and high—

plunder for us now
those still bright realms
of sky.

סִים

Not miracle, but metaphor,
the pundits now say,
citing the bright machinations

of myth, a logical explanation
for everything—Moses' parted sea,
Joshua's stopped sun, Goliath

on his knees at David's feet.
Who could dare deny this name
evoked for conjuring such?

Listen: In the village of Medjugorge
above the craggy slopes of Apparition
Hill, the sun does more than shine—

it dances, spins, and bleeds
as Mary, 5:40 on the dot each day,
reveals herself to a cadre

of peasant youths in the loft
of old St. James. Their tender
lips move silent and young heads

nod as if in sure agreement
with someone not quite there.
Onlookers look and flockers flock,

the faithful click of their cameras
amazing the darkening
air.

עלמ

If the brain is merely
a radio, receptor
of the twin broadcasts
of Light and Dark, then
my mother kept hers tuned
both day and night
to the non-stop static airwaves
of Station HELL.

If ninety-nine things
were immaculate with her brood
she would pluck at that single
imperfection, the way
her own mother plucked
at the feathers of chickens
doomed for the old black pot.

She died swearing
the nurses, vigilant at her bed,
were *throwing off* on her—
her phrase for making fun,
demeaning, putting cruelly down.

Had she only known this name
evoked for ridding heart and mind
of bleak imaginings, she might
have been more like me.
The perfect girl she wanted
all along. Not at all obsessed
with despairing thoughts—

at least none of my own.
Just those of hers, after all
these years, I can't stop
dwelling on.

מהש

So this is the name
I might have called upon
when I needed
of my latest childhood ailment
to be healed. But who

in her right mind
would have chosen
in those days
to be rendered well?
The way my mother

pampered me, yes, loved
me more than all the rest
when I was ill. All day
her smooth hand grazed
my fevered brow, the clean

warm cloth tucked soft
between the poultice
she had rubbed into my chest
and the flannel gown
I'd lounged inside

for days. Finally
just the two of us—
the others packed off
to school, my father
to the mill to pull

his double shift. And always
my mother's ironing board
erected close to my
couch-turned-into-bed.
Steam rose like angels

from my father's khaki
shirts as the days
of other people's lives
flickered their bright

promise across the black

and white. *My stories,*
she called them, the only thing,
she claimed, that kept her
sane. She didn't know
the word *sane* meant *health.*

Neither did I until years
later, French 101, when
the teacher demonstrated
for us all a proper Parisian
toast. *A votre sane,* she spoke

in her most elegant dialect,
then raised a ghostly vessel
to the class. *To your health,*
in any language, this name
of God proclaims.

The only name I know
to call upon, now
that she is gone.

ללה

Like receiving a letter from God
and not bothering to open it,
a friend once replied, when I spoke

of the nightly congregation of dreams
I tended to ignore. Kabbalah, too, affirms
our dreams yet another name for God,

name that journeys us each night
to the place where water runs uphill
and people fly. Each a divine gratuity.

Counselor or little priest. Doctor attending
patient to our ills. But what of the night
you peered into that mirror to find your eye

no longer just an eye, but a bright bright
bright aquarium. How the seaweed ribboned,
bannering upwards toward the water's

silvery surface and the little fish that swam
in their rosy stippled skins, bubbling air like
rainbowed baubles from their gills. Back and

forth, forth and back they went and you loved
them and missed them when you woke, ran
to the mirror dismayed to find your eye

only an eye again—iris of palest blue,
cornea lashed with ordinary lash,
dark pupil a small stopped sun devoid

of any light. Yet years later, when doubt
shadows like a pall, remorse and guilt
and shame for all you might have been,

you conjure again that night, wrap yourself
in the realm of dream where your eye, if only
for a moment, was more—oh so much

more—than just a human eye.

אבא

After the towers
    have tumbled,
        after the day's
    good weaving
undone   undone   undone
        the little Pompeii's
    of our daily lives
reduced to shard and ash
    this is the name
        that will right
it all again

the villagers rising startled
to their dusty feet
as if from an ancient sleep.

And see how the frayed
threads gather, mend their
tattered way into the warp
and weft of some long-ago
promised shroud.

Yes, this is the name
that will raise again the beams,
conjure the girders' strength,
render whole the shattered window
panes, calling back into essence
the bright fragmented brilliance
of our lost selves.

כהת

We dreaded passing,
those Halloweens,
Ora Snipes's house,
that ramshackle porch
she held vigil on, feet
propped against the peeling
rail, chair teetering
on its hind legs
just far enough
not to let her fall, the gun
we'd heard rumor of
resting in her lap
like a child she loved,
just waiting for those of us
she didn't to step one scrawny
foot beyond the boundary
of her drive. We'd seen her

from another distance, watching
beyond the school yard's chain-link
fence, her hair a tattered web
of gray, old face the glaciered plain
that stared back each day
from the worn front covers
of our science books. We dreaded

and could not stop ourselves
from passing there, could feel,
the closer we approached, the air
around us change, as if some unseen
weight secured her guarded
house of emptiness. Had we held

in our small lexicons this name
of God, we could have stepped
there anyway—sure and light—
feeling the leaden air
dissolve, revealing the gun
for what it really was—nothing
more than a ready cache
of apples, lollipops, and gum.

A Sentimental Education

Language: A Sentimental Education

How it makes and breaks you.
That tenuous stringing together
of letters and sounds. *Mean* and *amen*.
Casual and *casualty*.
Good and *god* and *dog*.

How it can turn on you.

The way my first grade teacher's eyes
bulged in disbelief
the day I ran crying to her,
tattling on the snot-nose boy
who had poked me
in my boll-weevil
with his pencil.

I can feel the mortification
of that moment still,
the class tumbling
into hysterics,
collapsing
among the jacks
and pick-up sticks
as I lifted my shirt for her to see,
the whorls of my primordial wound
reddening where his eraser had gone.

"It's time," my mother said
as I recounted, later, the sequence
of events. *Time*, she said, and began
the inevitable cleansing,
slow evacuation

of the beautiful rhetoric of metaphor she had six years
blessed me with.
That day she gave me *navel.*
The next, *vagina* and *urinate.*
Words that could take me anywhere.

Help me, she assured,
disappear into any crowd.

Good dog.

ABATTOIR

The first time I heard the word
I imagined some faraway room
too lavish and exotic for the likes
of me. Mounds of velvet pillows,
beds carved and fluffed and canopied,

fringed shades to ease the blinding
noonday sun. In seventh grade
I was taught to get to the root of things,
all the *oirs* of our daily lives waiting
to be deciphered—*Boudoir, armoire,*

reservoir—places where things of value
might safely be kept. Chambers for dreaming
ladies. Wardrobes lush with dresses, hats,
and gowns. Walled pools of clean, fresh
water to quench the browning crops.

But when that lost and lovely word
came floating back to me, I was shocked
to learn there was also a place for misery
and pain. For the once bright creatures

prodded down the line, wide-eyed,
mewling, blinking still, though the slashed
carotid, the quick, sure current of the stunning
rod had promised otherwise. How beautiful

it had sounded to me then. *Abattoir…*
Abattoir…Abattoir…. A place,
had I been invited, I might

have stepped lightly in.

WHERE'S MY FROG?

We worshipped her, Mrs. King,
who was ours for only half the day
that year. Sixth grade, our sights

on junior high and all those kids
from the good side of the tracks
she gave her mornings to

before driving to our dingy
neighborhood for history
and language arts. We

would have done anything
for her, as if having only half
rendered her more valuable,

the way we cherished our always
absent fathers, our mothers dull
in their faded aprons and always

tired, the most wretched
of commodities, being wholly
ours. One day she motioned me

to her desk, Lavon Deese, too,
a girl from up the street who'd
failed two grades, anathema

to all the other teachers whose
lessons she'd slumbered through.
The class was reading to themselves,

heads bent quiet above the hard
and colored history of our state.
We trembled on our way, the wood

beneath our soles creaking with every
step that delivered us to the vase
she'd lifted from her desk, huge globe

filled fresh each Monday with peonies
and mums, blossoms of magnolia
that rotted through the week

as the tests and essays grew,
an ominous Mt. Sinai next to them.
We couldn't believe she'd chosen us,

to deliver safely down the hall into
the girls' rest room that vase like
the holy-grail we'd learned about

at Saturday matinee, the sole purpose
of our common life now realized. In
the restroom the sun poured through

like the light in the painting my mother
had got with green stamps, Jesus offering
up his thorn-encrusted heart, the eyes

you could not escape no matter where
you sat. Into the rusty can we flung
the browning petals, their stems now limp,

leaves curled and brittling like the husks
of cicadas that signaled summer's end, then
into the nearest stall to flush beyond oblivion

the swampy dregs. When we eased into her
hands the empty vase, scrubbed and polished
to an astral sheen, our one breath stopped,

hungry for the smallest wafer of her
gratitude, stunned at what we got instead—
the slitted eye, stuck frown of her face

peering deep inside, those three bleak
words: *Where's my frog*? Our knees went
soft, the folds of our single brain calling back

the mysterious ker-plunk we'd heard
at the bottom of the commode
just as I pressed the lever.

The rest of that whole year we suffered
her disdain, we who had killed
her beloved pet, the one she brought

with her each Monday to bask
in the still primordial waters
of that week's blooms. Dark Lethe

my dreams would conjure, childhood's
defining act I would bear into the purgatory
of junior high Lavon decided to forego,

then high-school and on to college,
to the man I would finally marry,
who years later beneath the whirring

fan of an antique shop, would lift from its shelf
a small glass orb, the likes of which I'd never seen,
its surface a conglomeration of tiny holes,

and *Look,* he would say, as he handed it to
me...*a frog. I haven't seen one in years.*

I don't know what happened to Lavon.

Syntax

*Where haunts the ghost after the house
is gone?* I once wrote. First line of my first
poem in my first creative writing class. I'd
been reading Byron, Keats, and Shelly, lots
of Poe, loved how the cadence of their words
fit the morass my life had fallen to. I had
stayed up all night, counting stressed
and unstressed syllables, my mother's
weeping through the door of her shut room
echoing the metrics of my worried words.
It was the year our family blew apart,
my mother, brothers and sisters and I fleeing
in the push-button Rambler with no reverse
an uncle had taught me to drive. I loved that poem,
finally knew how words the broken and bereft
could alchemize, couldn't wait to get to class,
could hear already in my mind that teacher's
praise. When it came my turn to read, the paper
trembled in my hand, my soft voice cracked,
years passed before I reached the final word,
before she took the glasses from her nose
and cocked her head. *You've skewed your syntax
up* was all she said. I remember nothing else
about her class. That spring her house burned
down, she died inside. *Where haunts the ghost
after the house is gone?* I had several alibis.

First-Year Teacher

During an impassioned lecture
on the three principal parts
of *hang* and *hang*,
I turned from my grainy
etchings across the board
and in the voice
of a would-be pundit
whose moment had finally come,
said, "Please remember, class,
men cannot be hung."

The laughter began
a ripple down the aisle,
a prurient note
passed from desk to desk
until the entire class
let loose a roar.

When they finally gained composure
someone said,
"Couldn't it just be
you've had bad luck
with men?"

Found Poem

Beyond the parking lot of Jack's
Convenience Mart, halfway between
the clinic and Lincoln High, it finds

me, insinuates itself under the sole
of my left shoe, *Winter Poem* by Nikki
Giovanni, scrawled sloppily in ink

and torn from a spiral notebook. I shift
the sack of bread and milk to my right
hand, reach down and pick it up.

Once a snowflake fell
on my brow... the opening reads,
the script maintaining an artless

integrity that by line three
has already begun to falter... *& I*
loved it   slash   *so much I kissed*

it & it was happy   scribble slash....
Our teenage amanuensis seems to rally
here, writing through without an error

to the end. Following is an assignment
some teacher made—*Syntax Symbol Diction*—
like a doctor's clipboard checklist, a proper

diagnosis of the poem at hand. No
mention of the heart's terrain, words
that in one breath can break and mend,

render bright the tarnished world
below. How clever that young hand
to let it go.

An American Family

ST. PETER SAID, "THAT'S GOOD ENOUGH," AND HE WALKED THROUGH

After my father died, he came to me
in a dream, and in a voice, raspy, some
where between a bad Brando and Bogey,
asked if I would accompany him

to the gate, talk him into heaven. It was
cold. March. And night. I didn't
want to go, could think of nothing to advance
his cause, so rose sulking and petulant

and followed him. Saint Peter, flustered, got
out of bed. Name one good thing, he said, waiting.
Finally I recalled the mutilated dog
he once shot to put out of its misery.

We stood there at the weatherless gate, still
strangers, odd pair out of sync until…

The Sabbatical

The year my niece grew
ashamed of me, I lived
in a hidden cabin

on my sister's farm—I
who had been the magical
aunt, treasured exotic kin

in the faraway city she could
vanish to for long, lazy weekends
or months at a time in summer,

lunching in grown-up restaurants,
foraging the aisles of bookstores,
museums, and fragile shops

where she alone of all
earth's little girls could touch, beneath
her aunt's protective gaze, anything

she wanted, her fingers soft,
lifting then lighting along the shelves
of antique dolls and porcelain thimbles,

the expensive, loved possessions
of the now long dead. And always
I would catch in my rear-view mirror

the kiss she blew as I pulled out,
having delivered her home again.
How dare I take it all away, come

bumping and rattling into the humdrum
days of her world, lugging behind me
the contents of my own—reduced, even

as she watched, to a single room
where morning until dusk I would languish
in the crumpled gloom of words.

It didn't help she was about to turn
thirteen, her lone ambition painless
initiation into the teenage realm

of cool. It didn't help when the birthday
sleepover girls crept against her
protestations down the weedy path

to witness the strange woman
they'd heard was living there.
I must have seemed

the witch they thought they'd left
behind in the childhood mist
of make-believe: the way, beyond

the window's dim-lit frame, I hovered
at my desk—a cauldron for all they knew,
a doubling bubbling stew of frog

and newt, seasoned thick
with the delicate sweet bones
of their kind. And what of the broken

commode I had dragged from the creek
into my yard and filled with petunias
and ferns, the jars of burgeoning

sprouts along the sill they mistook,
I later learned, for grubs and worms?
Months would pass before she spoke

to me again, before the soft knock
at my cabin door, she on the stoop
asking to borrow the silver hoops

finally in style once more.
She wouldn't come inside or look
at me, as if not looking meant I wasn't

there at all, but back, still, in the distant
gilded land of fairy tale and dream.
When I placed the glittering circles

in her outstretched palm, I saw how her
blonde hair had caught in the maze
some spider had spun over night.

Cool Radio

When she calls and asks
if I will drive her to the mall,
our city's newest labyrinth

of glittering stuff, I know my sister
has come back to me, back
from November's shock of blood,

the exams, the x-rays, the surgeon's
winnowing blade. She is one week
out of the hospital, chemo bag

draped casually across her shoulder,
spilling its slow promise
into her veins. Odd how stylish

in the mall's fluorescent lights,
A Gucci or Von Furstenburg,
its pale blue plastic shiny

as the toy shoes and purses
we used to play grownup in.
I loop my left arm through her

frail right, her tired gate lanky,
almost chic, steady her against
the teenage throng, tattooed

and pierced and spiked, past
racks of skirts and dresses, tier
upon tier of stiletto heels

like the ones our dead mother
in her younger years
suffered so beautifully in.

At the base of the escalator,
beyond The Limited and The Gap,
a girl too young for fashion's

fleeting realm spies the apparatus
around my sister's neck. "Cool
radio," she whispers to no one

as we all step on together.

AN AMERICAN FAMILY

At the grocery store I bought pumpkins,
one for each of us—me, my husband,
and our blond daughter—so I might teach her
the lost art of family, art of mothering

earth, pies a spice cloud from the oven
and the solace of seeds, those tiny
purses of goodness spilling their best kept
secret into our mouths: nothing, nothing

ever lost or wasted. The picture we must
have made there! The little ghost bears
of our breath just out of their summer caves
and the maple loosing its yellow stars

onto our sweaters and hair. I couldn't stop
myself, as we chiseled our lovely symmetry
of mouths and noses and eyes, couldn't stop
imagining a chopper humming over, the surprised

photographer from, say, *Family Life*, leaning
precariously out to freeze the scene forever.
It was then I noticed they weren't carving
at all, the two of them laughing and giggling

as they hammered acorns for eyes into the pulpy
flesh, the grotesque slurs of mouths
a deranged arrangement of brackets and nails
scavenged from the shed, each fat orange

head complete with cornhusk rolled
cigar, a toupee of dead chrysanthemums.
So this was the thanks I got! My Happy Jack
next those creatures my husband

and daughter had dubbed Crack Kills
and Syndrome. A scene more likely
to be caught by some hack from *National
Enquirer*, our story relegated to an inside

page, obscured by the juicier "Man Dies
at Ninety: Pooch Serves as Pall Bearer."
What should I care? If the truth be known,
there were no sweaters and the day

unseasonably warm. My daughter's hair
not blond at all, but the brown bark
of the oak whose stubborn leaves cling
like dirty laundry to its branches,

her father and I living
in sin, bound straight for hell
as his mother continues to warn—
that woman who named me

for the slut I guess, after all, I am.

All Adverbs, Adjectives Too

Odd thing, I thought,
   for a teenager to say she
      despised. The hair-do

of the girl at the table
   next to us I might have
      understood. Or the jock

who yesterday between
   biology class and history
      took back his ring. But why

this sudden announcement
   at the height of our weekly
      outing over burgers and shakes?

I was not her blood,
   but that oddest of creatures,
      soft surrogate body designated

step, the woman loyalty to her
   mother required that she
      hate. How else, in her logic,

to remind me of that? I who
   worshipped at The Church of God
      of Rhetoric, lone walker through

the valley of the shadow of
   words. I watched her face drain
      pale, the laughter fade, fat heart

of a strawberry stopped midair
   between her fingertips and tongue.
      And then that cruel pronouncement,

adamant declaration spewed my way
   in the midst of our frivolity, sending
      me once again to my proper place.

No sooner had she spoken than the light
   returned, the strawberry resuming its
      journey through her penitent lips.

I held a second longer
   the feigned hurt across my face,
      vowed never to let her know

I despise them too.

The Napkin

One night in a pub
on the outskirts of Roanoke,
I sat with my husband

at a table lit only
by the candle's mute flickering
and the small waning moons

of our drinks. I was writing
in my journal, journaling
a journey soon coming

to its end when suddenly,
at the table to our left,
a soft commotion of arms

and hands. I looked
at my husband, lost in some
lost moment of the now

lost day, and then at them,
a subtle, peripheral glance
I had long ago perfected.

I could easily have touched
them—they were that close—lovers,
perhaps, signing to each other

their tongueless words. Each
in turn, their hands rose, bright
wings above the flame's dim

corona, secret negotiations
of finger and thumb.
I was stunned to see

how beautiful he was, as if
in the convoluted logic
of my mind, those devoid

of sound and speech must, too,
be devoid of loveliness.
I could see the silvery sheen

of her nails, glimmer of bracelets
and rings as they mounted the air,
lifting then falling, strafing

the crumbed and waxy
landscape of the table below.
When they left, something

fluttered to the floor, the napkin
they had at intervals been scribbling
on, passing back and forth,

the sweet lexicon of their
hands eluding even them.
My husband reached down,

handed it to me. Slowly
I began to read,
unfolding like lingerie

the delicate layers,
each boneless,
fleshless

syllable
naked before
my eyes: *She*

should be talking
to him, it said, *not writing*
in that book. Poor guy,

he looks so lonely.

Unmentionables

A Suit Our Brother Could Have Worn

In a family loyal to the ghost of our home state,
there's always the renegade

cousin. Old aunt who retreats
at Christmas. The turncoat niece.

Infantries of nephews
threatening to secede. And then to

secede from that. This time it was Mother,
who couldn't believe my sister

and I would darken the door
of that funeral home where

her own dead sister's husband
lay. Not one of them

had shown—not even a card—
when our darling brother

died. The two of us went anyway. Rendezvoused
at a store we knew

on the outskirts of our hometown where
nothing could have prepared

me for what happened there. For the way
my sister turned to me, seized both my

just-washed hands and pressed
them without warning to her burgeoning breasts.

What leap of time and space,
not to mention faith,

had catapulted me to the toilet of the Stop & Save where
I now stood, caressing my younger sister?

She who all her life had prayed for ampleness.
Whose padded bra I'd poke in jest

if she walked past and Mother wasn't looking. Whose
flesh rose now like jellied mounds

beneath my startled palms. Later we were shocked
to see our uncle lying there so small, not

half the man he used to be in a suit our
brother could have worn.

Our dry-eyed cousins seemed perplexed when we
began to weep, nieces—not even blood—shaking

in each other's arms above a bible made of papier-mache
and flanked in plastic mums. Finally

someone spoke to comfort us—*You know, he always
could've stood to lose a little weight.*

On our drive back to the Stop & Save, my
sister blew her nose and wiped her eyes

then reached inside her dress and pulled
them out, two small

sacs of silicone she'd ordered on the internet.
These things are killing me, she said,

and rolled her window down. Sometimes I wonder,
still, what passed through the stranger's

mind who found them lying there.

The Living Daylights

She'd beat it out of all
of us, she warned, if we
dared defy her rules,

tried her thinning patience
one more time. Truth is, she
never laid a hand on anyone,

though once, for some small
forgotten truancy, she snatched
me without warning from my play,

swatting at my behind
with a belt she'd grabbed
from its too-convenient hook

on the closet door, and oh
what a sight together there
we made, round and round

the living room, a windmill,
top, fine whirligig, bright wheel
and she the axis to my screeching

spoke. By the time she finally
ceded me the win, not a lick
had grazed the small but quicker

shins that carried me bruise-free
into womanhood, I who fared
no worse than the neighbor kids

who bore into the world deep marks
of defter hands. She's gone
now, benign and hopeless queen

of discipline, the living daylights
beaten, in the end, out of all of us.

Unmentionables

Odd how my mother's incessant utterings
seemed only an attempt
to unsay the world her eyes,

her ears, her nose, her ever-flitting
hands bore witness to. *Unthinkable,*
unspeakable, unheard of, she would

say, annihilating the bits
and pieces of unpalatable news
that daily came her way.

That unfortunate down the street, she
dubbed the woman who traded
herself for cash to feed

her hungry brood. And the ultimate
obscuring, total obliteration
of the offending word—*unmentionables,*

meaning the clean cotton panties
my sisters and I wore beneath
the pique and organdy

of our dresses and skirts. Sundays
at dinner, it was always
drumstick, dark meat, trotter

she would ask someone to pass,
the word *leg* far too erotic
for her lexicon. Had she not gone

when she did, this is what they would
have done to her: amputate her lower
extremities, or, as the doctor

later, so clearly, put it—cut off
both her legs. How considerate
the gods to have spared her

the indelicacy of those words,
mortification of a different kind.

Death has no manners, Mama—
unspeakable, unthinkable, unutterable—

that unfortunate down the street,
waiting, in the soft, ephemeral
lure of her unmentionables.

SHADOW DANCING

I wish Miss Saylo could've seen
the night my brother said, *Go Limp*,
then swirled me in his arms across

the discotheque, light and lithe,
more graceful than I had ever been,
she who'd put an end to my dancing

days. She was tiny and all pruned up,
like those photos I never understood
of vegetables dressed like people,

ribbed peppers sporting glasses,
tomatoes in tutus and tiaras. She
carried a big stick, nudged to attention

our clavicles and ribs if we slouched
in our pliés or rendered too soft
our arabesques. I tried to do what she

instructed. Pretended to be that leaf
fluttering from its tree, oh, down
and twirling down I went, landing

in a tangled mass amidst the fine
and tutored elegance of the other girls.
When she shouted, *Stop!* it took a moment

to realize she was talking to me,
though grace of some sudden other
kind made her wait until later

to relegate me to the stool
by the record player
where until semester's end

I would raise and lower the needle
at her command. So it was she
I thought of years later,

in the unschooled pedagogy
of my brother's arms, beautiful
in his white suit, the pink shirt

with pearl buttons he would keep
for years, long after the disease
had ravaged him, the Bus Stop

and the Hustle having entered, too,
oblivion's faithful realm. *Go
limp*, was all he said, and I did,

each lift and trill of the Bee Gees'
bright falsettos waking the long
muted language of my body.

Even Andy was not dead yet.

MY BROTHER'S STAR

I'm healed, my brother said,
his voice trembling, small quakes
of joy through the wires

connecting the ghostly morning
of his far coast with the early afternoon
of mine. It was late August. I wanted

so badly to believe, I let myself.
I who'd begun to pray for miracles,
the urgency of my pleas

rising exponentially with the slow
sloughing off of his white cells.
When I saw him in September,

he seemed even more diminished,
though he said it again—*I'm healed.*
Again and again he said it, at

the oddest times. To the cashier
in the florist shop when he ordered
roses for the doctors he would no

longer need. Once I heard him
whisper it to the juniper in his back
yard. The leaves, I swear, began to flutter

though there was no breeze. As I
was packing to fly home again, he led
me to his closet, took from its wire

hanger his most beautiful shirt
and handed it to me, the sweet smell
of his dwindling body draped now across

my arms. In October his St. Christopher
traveled back with Allen. With Rosie,
his favorite robe. But when Tricia

came home with his star, spikes
of golden sheen haloed in silvery
dust, cherished ornament he placed

each year atop his Christmas tree, I
began to scream. Into the startled face
of the sister I adored. November.

He had given her his star.

And I knew, finally, what
my brother meant. What he meant
when he said, *I'm healed.*

And began giving his things away.

QUESTIONS FOR PLUTO

QUESTIONS FOR PLUTO

Did the authorities
knock, too,
at your door,
the sun
you had always
counted on
not yet
fully risen
to his high place?

And who was that man,
hard, cold star
pinned
to the midnight blue
of his chest,
telling,
yes, telling you
you were not,
after all,
who you thought
you were.

Last Day

For Kate Berryman

Readying for the morning errands, you bundled
baby Sarah, Martha off already
to her daily dose of history, language arts.
You won't have to worry about me
anymore, he said, donning a coat and scarf. You'd heard it
all before, who'd born him to exhaustion, loved him well.

I, too, shopped that morning, met my husband
later at KFC—2 wing deals, 2 sweet teas—
where beyond the rippling window that sudden first white.
It's snowing! I gasped. *Spitting,* he corrected, as like
a school girl lured from the day's unfinished lessons,
I pressed my nose to the glass.

That night, wine and the gas logs blazing, Keillor on the radio
reading your husband's poem. How had he done it, my
husband wanted to know when I mentioned the suicide.
And in my happy ignorance so began
the stunning last revision
of his plan.

The Notes

for Nick Flynn

You dreamt your mother's
scrawled in pencil on a brown paper bag,
and in the bag, huddled at the bottom, six baby mice.
Ah, but the care my husband took!
Classic font laid meticulously down
against the finest bond,
brandished,
even,
with epigraphs.
Twice that week he'd interrupted the morning's work
to solicit my better memory—a couplet
of rich prosody, resonant line of prose. Words,
throughout the single decade of our love,
the two of us had cherished, I unwitting
collaborator of his final masterpiece.
You dreamt the bag
smoldering
from the top down
as your mother's voice
released into the night.
Dreamt the mice growing wilder
as it burned,
their only way out,
if ever,
through the fire.

How It Is In Their Clothes

for Maxine Kumin

A month after your friend's death
you put on her blue blazer, dipped
your hand into the left pocket
to find only a hole, in the right
a parking ticket
plucked from the windshield
of her old sedan, truant car
that would idle later
at the scene
of her final
crime.

Three seasons before I could touch
my husband's clothes, take them down
from their racks, slip my body
into the arms of the handsome
tweed I had loved him in.
I, too, foraged each pocket.
In the right, a single fortune
cookie, hermetically

sealed still in cellophane.
In his left,
as in hers,
a hole.

To Nicholas and Frieda Hughes

O, little birds, what was it like
falling, that night,
to sleep, your beds
the warm, safe nests

she had made for you, her face that would
finally fade
like details of
the fairy tale

she had weaned you on. And how did
it feel, unfeath-
ered, still, that long-
est other fall-

ing?

SOLACE

Each morning in my mailbox
or tucked into a quiet cove
of my front porch, another
burden of solace
reminding me again
my husband is dead.

Last week, an oval cardboard box
decoupaged in stars, inside, its nested
offering—a cache of still-warm eggs
gleaned from my neighbor's henhouse.

Yesterday, a Peruvian prayer shawl,
the warp and weft of its holy weave
climbing, like girders of a bridge,
its sturdy warmth.

And today this handmade flute,
turned and hollowed and carved
by Laughing Crow, enigmatic
shaman of some distant plain.

See its little row of holes
lined up like perfect planets,
as if having not yet learned
the universe had collapsed.

See my lips pressed to the tiny
breathless gape of its own mouth.
As if my lungs could conjure anything.
As if it were the one needing to be saved.

Whistle-Speak

Three weeks after your death
I found them, dog-eared,
flagged and marked, colorful
brochures you had hoped

to tempt me with, a trip
you'd planned for years
to that tiny drift of islands
courting Africa's golden

cheek. Remnants of old
volcanoes, fallen ash
and chard, each island
a realm of gorges and ravines

radiating from their centers
like spokes of a wheel. Who
wouldn't want to go there,
where the second native language

is that of birds, shepherds whistling
their messages to an ear cocked miles
away. Where even insults mimic
the mating songs of doves. See

how this old denizen folds his little
finger, presses tight against his tongue
and blows, free hand a makeshift
megaphone cupping conjured sound,

a trill, a chirp, a squawk
surfing the crags and slopes
of no man's land. *It can be used
for anything,* the caption reads:

Call to your friend.
Gather home your children.
Find, in a crowd, the husband
you've somehow lost.

Pear Moonshine

for Sue Campbell and Candy Butler

One night, the darkest winter of my life,
my husband not three cycles dead, I
opened the kitchen door to a quiet knock

and there in the starless gloom
of my back porch, two women bearing
gifts. In Candy's outstretched hands

a pot of homemade soup, in Sue's,
a jar of swollen pears embalmed
in liquid fire. When I reached

to fetch three tumblers down, the two began
to laugh, removed the offending vessels
from my startled hands and returned

them to their rightful place again. Sue
led me to the living room by the hearth
as Candy spun the gold corona

of its lid, drank deep and passed
the jar to Sue then on to me, the ghostly
triad of our lips leaving their own

soft crescents along the rim. Outside
no star had yet to show, no other
moon to light the snow that all day

long had kept me weeping close
to the sputtering flames. We drank
and passed the waning jar and drank

again until the glacier of my pain
began to break, a thousand icy floes
drifting down the river of my grief

and then we ate the soup.

NOTES

I am indebted to Rabbi Yehuda Berg whose book *The 72 Names Of God: Technology for the Soul* provided me some understanding of the teachings of *The Kabbalah*. According to Rabbi Berg these names of God, each represented by three Hebrew letters, designate energies that come into the world with us at birth and remain with us on a soul-level throughout our lives. The first section of *The Candle I Hold Up to See You* attempts to explore some of these names *for* God in a poetic and particular way.

"Questions for Pluto" (p. 77) alludes to the 2006 declaration by certain scientists that Pluto is too small to be considered a planet.

"Last Day" (p. 78) is addressed to Kate Berryman, wife of the poet John Berryman who committed suicide by jumping from a bridge in 1972.

"The Notes" (p. 79) is a response to Nick Flynn's poem "Bag of Mice" that alludes, ostensibly, to his mother's suicide note.

Nicholas and Frieda, of the poem "For Nicholas and Frieda Hughes," (p. 80) refer to the two small children of the poet Sylvia Plath, who committed suicide in 1963.

"How It Is In Their Clothes" (p.81) is a response to Maxine Kumin's poem "How It Is In Your Clothes," a poem that alludes to the suicide in 1974 of her close friend Anne Sexton.

Colophon

This book was set in Abobe Caslon. William Caslon released his first typefaces in 1722. Caslon's types were based on seventeenth-century Dutch old style designs, which were then used extensively in England. Because of their incredible practicality Caslon's designs met with instant success. Caslon's types became popular throughout Europe and the American colonies; printer Benjamin Franklin hardly used any other typeface. The first printings of the *American Declaration of Independence* and the *Constitution* were set in Caslon. For her Caslon revival, designer Carol Twombly studied specimen pages printed by William Caslon between 1734 and 1770.

The image on the cover of this book is based on a painting, by baroque Dutch painter Godfried Schalcken (1643–1706) entitled *Pygmalion and Galatea*. Schalcken, early in his career, spent three years in the studio of Gerard Dou, one of the most famous students of Rembrandt. This artist, working at the end of the Golden Age of Dutch Painting, is most famous for his candlelight scenes. *Pygmalion*, is oil on a wood panel, and has been in its current location, Room 44 (The Rembrandt Room) at the Uffizi Gallery in Florence, Italy, since 1784.

— Chris Bartol

CATHY SMITH BOWERS was born and reared, one of six children, in the small mill town of Lancaster, SC. She received her BA and MAT in English at Winthrop University in Rock Hill, SC. She went on to do graduate work in Modern British Poetry at Oxford University in England.

Cathy Smith Bowers' poems have appeared widely in publications such as *The Atlantic Monthly, The Georgia Review, Poetry, The Southern Review,* and *The Kenyon Review.* She is a winner of The General Electric Award for Younger Writers, recipient of a South Carolina Poetry Fellowship, and winner of The South Carolina Arts Commission Fiction Project. She served for many years as poet-in-residence at Queens University of Charlotte where she received the 2002 JB Fuqua Distinguished Educator Award. She now teaches in the Queens low-residency MFA program.

Smith Bowers is the author of three collections of poetry: *The Love That Ended Yesterday in Texas* (TEXAS TECH UNIVERSITY PRESS, 1992), *Traveling in Time of Danger* (IRIS PRESS, 1999), and *A Book of Minutes* (IRIS PRESS, 2004).

LaVergne, TN USA
19 April 2010
179793LV00004B/71/P